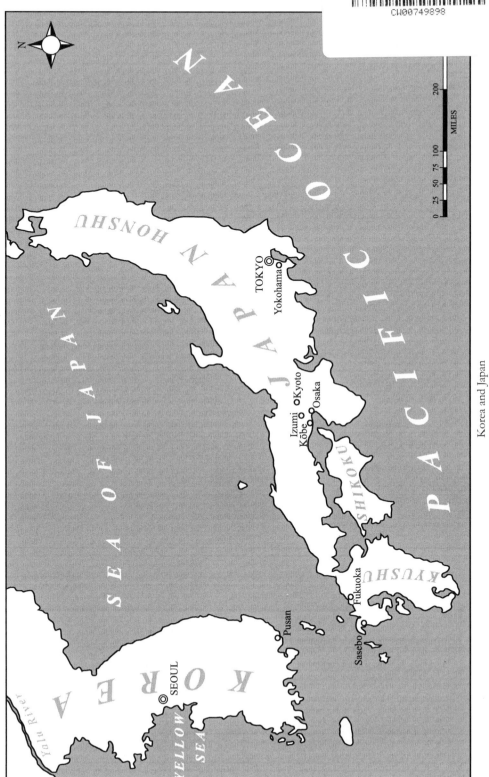

Korea and Japan

41 INDEPENDENT COMMANDO RM

KOREA 1950 TO 1952

BY

LT COL PETER THOMAS RM

SERIES EDITOR
CAPT DEREK OAKLEY MBE RM

ROYAL MARINES HISTORICAL SOCIETY
SPECIAL PUBLICATION NO 8

41 INDEPENDENT COMMANDO RM: *KOREA 1950–1952*
Copyright © Royal Marines Historical Society 1985

978 1 908123 01 5

First published 1985 by the
ROYAL MARINES HISTORICAL SOCIETY
Royal Marines Museum
Eastney
Southsea
Hants PO4 9PX
United Kingdom

Second Edition Published 1990
Reprinted 2008
Third Edition Published 2011

Printed and bound by CPI Group (UK) Ltd, Croydon, CR0 4YY

Contents

Acknowledgements

The author acknowledges the help of former members of 41 Independent Commando Royal Marines in compiling this short history, particularly the Commanding Officers: Colonel D B Drysdale DSO OBE and Major General F N Grant CB, who corrected and approved the drafts.

This book is an updated and improved edition of the Royal Marines Historical Society Special Publication No 8 which was first published in 1985. It contains many new photographs as well as those previously published

Many of the photographs were taken with a private camera by Corporal Les Coote, of the Intelligence Section, who kindly provided reprints for this revised edition.

Glossary of Illustrations

Chapter One

Introduction

Background

The Korean peninsula measures 600 miles from north to south and varies between 120 and 350 miles wide. To the north, across the Yalu River, lies Manchuria and the Russian port of Vladivostok is but ninety miles from its north east boundary. Across the Straights of Korea to the south lies Japan with the Sea of Japan to the east and the Yellow Sea to the west.

A mountainous range traverses the length of the peninsula, precipitous on the eastern side with 8,000 foot peaks in the north swept by the icy winds from the Manchurian plateau. The east coast has a negligible tidal range whilst on the west the range is as much as thirty-six feet. One of the main north/south lines of communication is the railway line which runs in and out of tunnels along the east coast between Hamhung and Chongjin. This was to become the target for most of 41 Commando's raids.

From 1910 Korea was administered as an integral part of Japan. At the Cairo conference in November 1943 the western allies pledged to make Korea a free and independent state but, when Russia belatedly entered the war against Japan, an arbitrary line was drawn across the 'waist' of the peninsula at the 38th parallel of latitude to denote the demarcation between Russian and US Forces to facilitate the Japanese surrender. When the Iron Curtain rang down around the Communist bloc this artificial boundary divided Korea into the Peoples Democratic Republic in the north, a Soviet satellite, and the Republic of Korea (RoK) in the south, a protégée of the United States.

The North Korean Peoples Army (NKPA) was armed, equipped and trained on the Soviet model but by contrast the RoK forces were relatively lightly equipped by the US for gendarmerie duties.

After a succession of border incidents and increasing bellicosity, the NKPA launched an invasion of South Korea with eight divisions, spearheaded by T34 tanks, on 25 June 1950. In a short time the NKPA had swept the few remaining RoK and US Army forces into the south east corner of the peninsula where they invested the Pusan perimeter.

Meanwhile the US achieved the 'uniting for peace' resolution in the United Nations General Assembly, which by chance Russia was boycotting, and member nations began contributing land, sea and air forces to restore the integrity of South Korea.

The British Pacific Fleet was committed to the UN and operated mainly on the west coast, whilst the US 7th Fleet's responsibility included the east coast which lent itself to amphibious operations.

Admiral Sir Patrick Brind, commanding the British Pacific Fleet, offered the Commander UN Naval Forces, Admiral C T Joy USN, a small raiding force to operate against the Communist lines of communication. As 3 Commando Brigade was already heavily engaged in the anti terrorist campaign in Malaya this committed the Corps to raising a small Commando unit for operations in Korea.

INWARD TELEGRAM

D.1912

File No.

From :— **British Embassy Rangoon**

Cypher
Code
Clear **Cypher**

To :— **Ukrep Karachi.**
Repeated Saving Foreign Office and Singapore.

Time of Despatch : 1/9/50

Time of Receipt : 1/9/50 (1710 1ST)

Originators No. 71 SECRET IMMEDIATE

Three BOAC Charter aircraft carrying Royal Naval personnel will pass through Karachi at approximately 0001 hours on September 4th September 5th and September 6th.

2. Grateful if you would arrange for following message to be delivered in writing to Senior Officer of each party. BEGINS

From Naval Attache Rangoon. It is most important from security aspect that you and your party should do all you can not to attract attention in Rangoon. You will be staying overnight at principal hotel and will have to be careful to avoid giving the impression of a large British service party.

Please explain this to your party en route. I will meet plane on arrival. ENDS.

Formation

41 Independent Commando RM, commanded by Lieutenant Colonel D B Drysdale, was formed on 16 August 1950 at Bickleigh Camp. Initially the unit comprised three separate groups; volunteers from UK establishments who were flown out by BOAC to Japan in plain clothes; some volunteer sailors and marines from the British Pacific Fleet, these were already in training when the UK contingent arrived and formed a rifle section known as the Fleet Volunteers; and a reinforcement draft destined for 3 Commando Brigade, aboard the troopship *Devonshire*, which was diverted to Japan by air via the Philippines.

The unit assembled at Camp McGill, a US Army post at Hayame near the US Naval Base of Yokosuka. 41 Commando was to be under US Naval operational command and was supplied, armed and equipped by the Americans. The first task was to train each component, as it arrived, on US weapons (see Appendix A) and raiding techniques (Appendix B).

Lieutenant Peter Thomas (the author) in Japan in 1950

Inspection of British Pacific Fleet volunteers by Lieutenant Angus MacDonald USMC, who was originally assigned to train the Fleet Volunteers and then lead them on operations as part of a US Army Ranger company. On Lieutenant Colonel Drysdale's arrival he was retained to train 41 Commando on US weapons, equipment and techniques. Lieutenant Pounds led the Fleet Volunteers on the Kunsan and Kimpo operations.

His Excellency the British Ambassador to Tokyo inspects 41 Independent Commando RM at Camp McGill.
Photograph by Les Coote.

Chapter Two

Early Raids

Background

With a bold stroke of military genius the Commander-in-Chief UN Command, General Douglas MacArthur, reversed the fortunes of the beleaguered UN forces by withdrawing the 1st Provisional USMC Brigade from the Pusan perimeter to form the 1st US Marine Division (1 Marine Division) at sea with two Regimental Combat Teams (or Brigade Groups) and HQ elements brought from the States. This fine Division made an amphibious landing at Inchon on 17 September 1950 and went on to seize the South Korean capital of Seoul. Simultaneously United Nations forces broke out of the Pusan perimeter. North Korean resistance started to collapse and their forces began to withdraw north of the 38th parallel.

41 Commando's Operations

As each part of 41 Independent Commando became operational it was despatched on operations. First POUNDFORCE comprising mainly the Fleet Volunteers, fourteen men under command of Lieutenant E G D Pounds, left in HMS *Whitesand Bay* to support the Inchon landings with a diversionary raid, as part of a US Army Raider battalion, on the west coast on 12/13 September. Subsequently the force joined 1 Marine Division for the Inchon landings on 17 September penetrating as far as Kimpo airfield before rejoining to participate in C and D Troops' raids.

Sixty-seven personnel of A and B Patrol, later to be organised into B Troop, accompanied by Lieutenant Colonel Drysdale, raided the east coast railway on 2 October from the troop carrying submarine USS *Perch* (1,526 tons); a converted BALAO class submarine with its torpedo tubes removed to make space for 110 troops. A cylindrical hangar abaft the conning tower carried a small power craft which could tow the rubber boats. On this raid anti-tank mines laid under the rails were heard to detonate during the withdrawal. Regrettably, a Royal Marine was killed during this raid.

125 men and five officers of C and D Troops, under command of the Second-in-Command, Major D L St M Aldridge, embarked in the Assault Personnel Destroyers USS *Bass* and *Wantuck* (1,400 tons). Each carried four Landing Craft and had accommodation for 162 in the troop space.

This force made two separate raids also against the east coast railway on 5 and 6 October 1950. The Assault Engineers laid two tons of charges on each raid under culverts and bridges and in tunnels. A Korean railway guard was killed and so, sadly, was a Royal Marines Corporal whilst leaving the beach on the second raid.

The journalist and MP, Tom Driberg, accompanied both these raids as a war correspondent and wrote a consolidated account in *Reynolds News*, a now defunct Sunday newspaper.

Burial at sea of Marine P R Jones from the submarine USS *Perch*.
Photograph by Les Coote.

On return from these raids 41 Independent Commando was reorganised (see Appendix C) and some useful unit and sub-unit training was conducted on the excellent field firing ranges on the slopes of Mount Fuji.

Training in Japan

On Parade at Camp McGill, Hayame

C Troop; Captain Bill Pearce and Lieutenant Jesse Haycock, at Camp McNair, Mount Fuji

Heavy Weapons Troop at Camp McGill

Chapter Three

Attachment to the
First US Marine Division

Background

Following the Inchon landings the 1st Marine Division was withdrawn and made two amphibious landings on the east coast in pursuit of the NKPA: at Wonsan and at Hung Nam. From there the Division under command of X Corps (Lieutenant General Almond USA) advanced seventy-eight miles into the mountains to the village of Udam Ni on the western arm of the Chosin Reservoir. (Eight Army, including the 27 and 29 Brigades, later the British Commonwealth Division, operated on the west of the peninsula).

In its 'Home by Christmas' euphoria the UN Command chose to disregard the ominous signs of Chinese intervention. Fierce attacks by Chinese Communist Forces (CCF) were reported against over extended UN units from late October but these ceased early in November as the Chinese reinforced and regrouped. Aerial reconnaissance showed massive troop movements across the Yalu River and China announced she would not stand idly by and watch her Communist neighbour overrun.

In the light of subsequent events a digression is relevant here to consider the attributes of the new enemy. The Chinese soldier crossed the Yalu armed initially with an assortment of Japanese, Russian and US (ex-nationalist) weapons and carrying some eighty rounds of ammunition and four days rations. Thereafter he was independent of routine re-supply. He wore a thick reversible yellow and white quilted cotton uniform and crepe soled canvas shoes. Inured to hardship, indoctrinated with communism, and by a 'hate America' campaign, and courageous to the point of being suicidal he made a formidable adversary.

This peasant army hid by day and made long approach marches by night. Adept at infiltration, mass attacks, almost invariably at night, were conducted by 'pepper potting' (small scale fire and movement) forward and exploiting every weakness and advantage. Coordination was achieved by bugles, whistles and flares.

The rapid advance of the UN Forces reduced opportunities for raiding and 41 Independent Commando was shipped to Hung Nam where it arrived on 15 November 1950, to be placed under command of 1 Marine Division and issued with cold weather clothing (Appendix A). The intention was for the commando, which (less a small rear

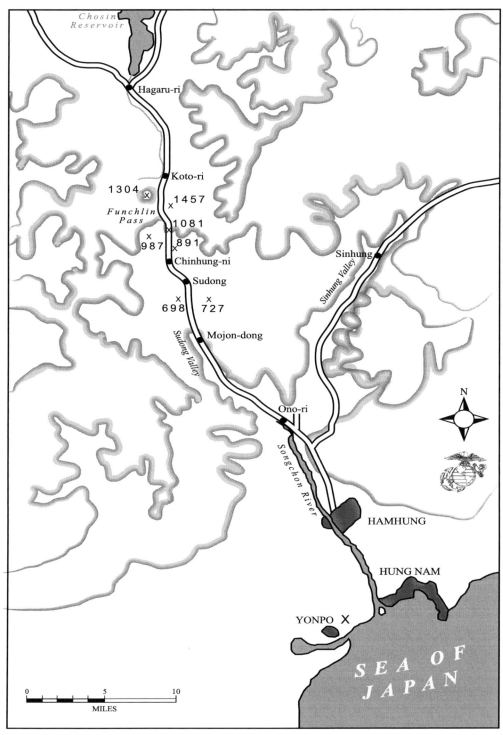

The Main Supply Route of the 1st Marine Division from Hung Nam to the Chosin Reservoir,
November – December 1950

The Second-in-Command, Major Dennis Aldridge, with the MO, Surgeon Lieutenant Dougy Knock, who was to be killed the next day. *Photograph by Les Coote*

B Troop in USMC trucks leaving Hamhung on 28 November 1950.
Photograph by Les Coote

party left in Japan) only mustered 235, to be used as an additional reconnaissance company to protect the left flank during the advance from Yudam Ni.

It should be noted that Major General O P Smith, commanding 1 Marine Division, had misgivings over the X Corps' plan to push him further out on a limb and into a winter campaign in the mountains. However, he managed to concentrate his division along the narrow single track road which was to become his vital Main Supply Route (MSR). He was thus in a better position to extricate his Division when the inevitable happened.

41 Independent Commando Operations with the First US Marine Division

After enjoying Thanksgiving Day at Ham Hung 41 Commando embussed in twenty-two 2½-ton trucks and one 30 cwt weapons carrier, contributed by divisional service units, for the journey up the line. (Only a Jeep had been allocated for the CO). This was to be an administrative move up the MSR and for ease of loading, stores, including heavy weapons, remained crated.

Breakfast at Koto-ri before advancing with Force DRYSDALE.
Photograph by Les Coote

Having driven to 4,000 feet up the Funchilin Pass the Commando arrived at Koto-ri where Colonel 'Chesty' Puller's 1st RCT HQ was based. The unit was greeted with the news that the CCF had blocked the road to the north and were given part of the perimeter to guard for the night.

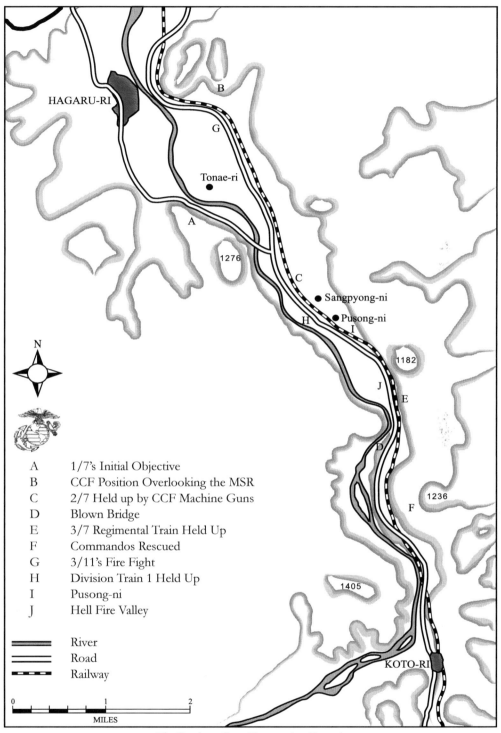

HAGARU-RI

B

G

Tonae-ri

A

1276

C

Sangpyong-ni

Pusong-ni

H

I

1182

J

E

D

1236

F

N

A   1/7's Initial Objective
B   CCF Position Overlooking the MSR
C   2/7 Held up by CCF Machine Guns
D   Blown Bridge
E   3/7 Regimental Train Held Up
F   Commandos Rescued
G   3/11's Fire Fight
H   Division Train 1 Held Up
I   Pusong-ni
J   Hell Fire Valley

━━━ River
═══ Road
▬ ▬ ▬ Railway

1405

KOTO-RI

0   1   2
        MILES

The Breakout from Hagaru-ri to Koto-ri,
6–7 December 1950

Early next morning HQ 1 Mar Div ordered that Task Force DRYSDALE, totalling 922 men and 141 vehicles, comprising: 41 Independent Commando, G Company 3 Battalion 1st Marines USMC, B Company 3 Battalion 31st Infantry US Army and elements of the Divisional train, be formed to fight its way to Hagaru-ri at the southern tip of the Chosin Reservoir.

There was just time for the Heavy Weapons group to break out a section of 81mm mortars and A4 Brownings before 41 Commando led the advance from Koto-ri at 0930 hours on 29 November 1950. Within two miles the Commando and G Company were up against serious resistance but at 1350 Force DRYSDALE was reinforced with seventeen tanks from D Company 1st USMC tank battalion which had moved up that morning. Slow progress was resumed until, at about 1615 hours, the column was halted four miles north of Koto-ri.

Lieutenant Colonel Drysdale asked Division HQ whether he should resume the advance and, because of the urgent need for reinforcements General Smith directed him to continue at all costs.

After a delay for the tanks to refuel, during which darkness fell, the advance resumed. The tanks declined to comply with Lieutenant Colonel Drysdale's request to spread in pairs throughout the convoy and pushed on to Hagaru-ri leaving the soft skinned vehicles unprotected.

About halfway to Hagaru-ri the MSR entered a defile where the CCF closed in and split the column, leaving one Heavy Weapons section, the Assault Engineers and elements of Commando HQ with most of B Company and Division HQ, who fought throughout the night, strung out in a number of defensive perimeters. Subsequently the Heavy Weapons section, led by Corporal E Cruse, found its way to Hagaru-ri badly frostbitten and seven of the Commando HQ personnel were led back to Koto-ri by the Assault Engineer Officer, Captain P J Ovens, after slipping out of the perimeter whilst surrender terms were being negotiated in the early hours of 30 November.

Meanwhile the remainder of the column forced on under sporadic fire until under a mile from Hagaru-ri where it was stopped by concentrated mortar and small arms fire within sight of the USMC Engineers working under floodlights to construct a 2,900 foot runway out of the frozen earth. The MSR was blocked by an abandoned tank and several vehicles were set on fire. During this phase Lieutenant Colonel Drysdale was slightly wounded and amongst the casualties were: BTp Commander Captain Parkinson-Cumine, the Medical Officer Surgeon Lieutenant D A Knock and Petty Officer J A Tate, section commander of the Fleet Volunteers, all killed; and D Troop Commander, Captain L G Marsh and the IO/Signals Officer, Lieutenant D L Goodchild, seriously wounded.

The last vehicles to enter the four mile defensive perimeter at Hagaru-ri were a 2½-ton truck and the Heavy Weapons 30 cwt, both loaded with wounded and led by

Captain Leslie Marsh RM

Lieutenant Gerald Roberts RM

the Heavy Weapons Officer Lieutenant P R Thomas. Force DRYSDALE had sustained 321 casualties and lost seventy-five vehicles, but to quote from the official USMC history, 'To the slender garrison of Hagaru-ri was added a tank company and some 300 seasoned infantry.' Less than 100 of 41 Independent Commando got through and sixty-one became battle casualties. Those who arrived are indebted to Lieutenant Colonel Beall, commanding the 1st Motor Transport Battalion, for taking them in and providing food and shelter from the sub-zero temperatures which at night fell to -24°F.

US and Royal Marines at Hagaru-ri waiting to move south

The author (right) at Hung Nam camp

41 Commando was nominated Garrison Reserve under command of 5 RCT (Lieutenant Colonel Murray). The first call came on the night of 30 November/1 December when B Troop, now led by Lieutenant G F D Roberts (the Adjutant), took part in a counter attack to regain G Company's left flank on East Hill. This dominating feature was critical to the defence of the perimeter and although the garrison of Hagaru-ri were not to know it, the CCF shot their bolt that night when their 58th and 59th Divisions incurred an estimated 5,000 casualties in two large scale assaults.

A supply drop at Koto-ri on 4 December 1950.
Photograph by Les Coote

Survivors from Force DRYSDALE returning to Koto-ri on 30 November 1950.
Photograph by Les Coote

A funeral service for 117 United Nations personnel, including members of
41 Independent Commando, at Koto-ri on 8 December 1950.
Photograph by Les Coote

Chapter Four

The Advance to the Sea

A number of UN formations had disintegrated under the CCF attack. To the west, Eight Army was withdrawing and X Corps commander placed all troops in the Chosin reservoir area under the operational control of 1 Marine Divison. Seventy-five percent casualties had been suffered by three US Army battalions east of the Reservoir in five days of attacks. Only 385 able-bodied survivors eventually reached Hagaru-ri across the ice, to be re-equipped and reorganised as a provisional battalion.

In a high level conference at Hagaru-ri X Corps commander authorised Major General Smith to destroy all equipment and fall back with all speed to Hung Nam. General Smith replied that his Division would fight its way out, bringing back all its heavy equipment and that movement would be governed by his ability to evacuate his wounded. As 'withdrawal' was not in the USMC vocabulary this operation was to be called 'The Advance to the South.'

The first task was to concentrate the 5th and 7th RCT's sixteen rifle companies and the artillery of the 11th Regiment, back the fourteen miles over the mountains from Udam Ni where they had been under ferocious attack since 27 November. This was accomplished by 4 December and members of 41 Independent Commando who were privileged to go out to the perimeter to meet them will have an abiding memory of the splendid US Marine Corps infantry marching into Hagaru-ri alongside their wounded after fighting for a week in numbing sub-zero temperatures driven by the screaming north wind.

The next day 41 Commando made an abortive foray to recover nine 155mm howitzers which had been abandoned when their tractors ran out of diesel. These were later demolished; the largest loss of the Udam Ni breakout.

Whilst the men of the 5th and 7th Marines recovered in Hagaru-ri, casualty evacuation and re-supply continued apace. By nightfall on 5 December 4,312 men, including twenty-five Royal Marines, had been evacuated by air and 537 reinforcements flown in.

The plan for the move from Hagaru-ri to Koto-ri was for 7th Marines to lead and 5th Marines (Lieutenant Colonel R L Murray), with 41 Commando attached to bring up the rear. The operation was to be supported by Navy and Marine aircraft from seven US Navy carriers; the dedication of the pilots of the cranked wing Corsairs who had already flown many close support sorties in the most appalling weather conditions has become legendary.

The advance started at dawn on 6 December. It took thirty-eight hours to move the 10,000 troops and over 1,000 vehicles the ten miles to Koto-ri against fierce attacks from the seven CCF Divisions which were now concentrated against 1 Marine Division.

Before marching out of Hagaru-ri Lieutenant Colonel Drysdale ordered a unit inspection which impressed the USMC. The Royal Marines custom of shaving daily despite the freezing weather had been greeted initially with derision but eventually the USMC conceded there was something in such outward signs of self-discipline.

En route the Unit dead were recovered to be buried in a mass grave for 117, including US Marines and Soldiers, at Koto-ri on 8 December. Here too Captain Ovens' party of seven was reunited bringing 41 Independent Commando's strength up to 150 (A mistaken report on page 298 of US Marine Corps Operations in Korea' refers to the 2/7th Marines rescuing twenty-two Royal Marines during this phase of the withdrawal who had been stranded in CCF dominated territory since the convoy had fought its way through on 29/30 November. This statement cannot be substantiated).

There was a pause before the advance towards Hung Nam could be resumed whilst steel trackway was airdropped to bridge a demolished culvert in the Funchilin Pass. 1st Battalion 1st Marines also fought its way up the pass from the south to seize the key heights dominating the Pass.

41 Commando moved out of Koto-ri in a snowstorm in the afternoon of 8 December with the task of holding the high ground overlooking the MSR during the night to guard against infiltration. Whilst away the faithful 30 cwt weapons carrier, the only unit transport besides the Commanding Officer's Jeep, slid off the road and was later demolished (A tribute to the loyal USMC driver, Corporal D Saunchegrow, was published in the February 1970 *Globe and Laurel*).

Next morning the Commando returned to relieve 3rd Battalion 1st Marines in the Koto-ri perimeter. The unit set off with the 5th Marines column to march the twenty-three miles to the Hung Nam bridgehead held by two US Army Divisions. At Majon-Dong the Commando embussed in trucks to be ferried down to the tented assembly area prepared in Hung Nam.

By 11 December the whole of 1 Marine Division was clear. As Major General Smith had promised the Division had come out fighting, bringing its wounded and most of its equipment. In the process it had inflicted a major defeat on the CCF, which had sustained an estimated 37,000 casualties from all causes, including the bitter sub-zero weather.

41 Commando embarked with 22,000 US Marines in transports assembled off Hung Nam and were shipped down to Pusan. From there the Unit was moved west along the coast by LCT to Masan to spend Christmas 1950 with 1 Marine Division.

41 Independent Commando withdrawing down the Funchilin Pass.
Photograph by Les Coote

Wretched North Korean refugees during the withdrawal from Koto-ri.
Photograph by Les Coote

A Map reproduced by kind permission of the *Daily Telegraph*

Sadly, the US Marines were deprived of Christmas drink because of political influences back home (the Women's Christian Temperance Union for instance blocked the Milwaukee brewers' donation of a million cases of beer to the US Forces in Korea). 41 Commando, however, received a large consignment of 'medical supplies' from its friends in the British Embassy in Tokyo which enabled the whole unit to splice the mainbrace on Christmas Day. Contact had also been made with the British Army base in Pusan (which kindly lent two 30 cwt vehicles) and NAAFI stores were obtained with which the Officers

41 Commando's high morale is demonstrated by these Marines of HQ Troop rejoicing in a can of tea presented during the long march from Hagaru-ri. Corporal Dave Brady stands behind the man holding the can.

Photograph by Les Coote

Mess threw a cocktail party. The Commando cooks showed they were as good at concocting canapés as they had been with rifles.

41 Commando had suffered ninety-three casualties and was particularly short of specialists: assault engineers, signallers, heavy weapons NCOs etc. It was therefore decided to withdraw the unit to Japan in January 1951 to await reinforcements and

'Old Faithful', Corporal Don Saunchegrow's 30 cwt weapon carrier

USMC saying farewell to 41 Independent Commando
as they leave Masan after Christmas 1950 on the way to Japan

The Commanding Officer's jeep at Hung Nam

41 Independent Commando RM at Ebisu Camp, Tokyo. Reinforcements are wearing light coloured jerseys.

to retrain and re-equip. It was with mixed feelings that the Royal Marines of 41 Commando left their USMC comrades who were shortly to go back into the line with the Eight Army, now well south of the 38th Parallel. Lieutenant Colonel Drysdale wrote in his report: 'This was the first time that the Marines of the two nations had fought side by side since the defence of the Peking Legations in 1900. Let it be said that the admiration of all ranks of 41 Commando for their brothers in arms was, and is, unbounded. They fought like tigers and their morale and esprit de corps is second to none.'

Note: For this action between 27 November and 11 December, 1st US Marine Division and the attached units were awarded the Presidential Unit Citation. The wording of the citation is at Appendix 1 of Volume III of *US Marine Operations in Korea*. 41 Commando was not listed in the original citation but subsequent representations by the US Marine Corps resulted in 41 Commando being included. The award was accepted on behalf of the Corps by our Captain General from the US Ambassador to the UK in 1957.

The Sorye Dong beach. The recce party reported 'just a few stones"!

Chapter Five

The Sorye Dong Raid

4 1 Independent Commando moved into Ebisu Camp in the suburbs of Tokyo in January 1951 and all ranks enjoyed a period of R & R (Rest and Recuperation). Later the Unit was transferred to HMAS *Commonwealth*, the Naval Base at Kure to re-equip, train and absorb reinforcements. Unfortunately the arrival of key specialists was delayed and the Commanding Officer became concerned that morale would suffer through prolonged inactivity so plans were made to mount a unit raid to cut the east coast railway, which was again being used to move supplies from Manchuria to Hung Nam. This was to be a daylight demonstration in force with very considerable support.

On 2 April 1951 twenty-one Officers and 256 Other Ranks of 41 Independent Commando embarked in the LPD USS *Fort Marion* (eleven LVT, five LVT(A) and three LC) and the APD USS *Begor* (four LC). The Gunfire Support Group comprised a cruiser and two destroyers. Air Support was available from the carriers USS *Boxer* and USS *Phillipine Seas*. Six minesweepers were to approach to within 2,000 yards of the beach. An SFCP (Shore Fire Control Party), a Tactical Air Support Party and an Underwater Demolition Team (UDT), to reconnoitre the beach, were attached to the Commando.

USS *Fort Marion*

After two rehearsals of the Amphibious Group the Force assembled off the objective area where proper consultations between the group commanders became possible for the first time on D-l, 6 April 1951.

Royal Marines landing in the Sonjin area to destroy railway lines

The east coast railway embankment. Assault Engineers place charges in the boreholes.

Thick fog postponed the landing and reduced the naval bombardment to two hours, but at 0805 on 7 April, D Troop landed from two LVTs (armoured amphibians) and by 0900 hours the covering force was in position ready for the Assault Engineers, aided by the MT Section, to begin work.

Earlier raids had been directed at culverts and bridges, which could soon be repaired, and tunnels, from which roof falls could easily be removed (ideally a train wrecked in a tunnel would block a line longest). On this raid the target was the embankment. Demolitions were carried out in four phases: first, sixteen shaped charges were blown to make boreholes, next each borehole was packed with eighty pounds of TNT which were detonated. This process was then repeated in the craters to produce a gap in the embankment 100 feet wide and sixteen feet deep. Finally fifty-five anti personnel mines were laid in the craters.

When mining was complete the withdrawal started and the last LVT left the beach at 1555 hours. The Commando had been ashore for nearly eight hours and, apart from a small group which fired at C Troop from long range, there had been no enemy activity, although an informer reported two divisions in Songjin, fifteen miles to the north. There were no landing force casualties but unfortunately five villagers had been killed and fifteen wounded. These were tended by the SBAs; apart from this the naval bombardment had inflicted only superficial damage.

The Commando disembarked at Yokosuka and was re-established in Camp McGill on 13 April from where sub-unit and unit training continued.

Detonation of the railway line

The demolished railway line

Chapter Six

Wonsan Harbour and Further Raids

A period of relative inactivity ensued whilst future operations and a possible return to 1 Marine Division were discussed (peace talks started during this time). Finally, it was decided to establish a forward operating base on Yo-Do Island within Wonsan Harbour, some sixty miles behind the lines, and a Rear HQ in an old Japanese sea plane base near Sasebo, the HQ of Flag Officer Second-in-Command British Far East Fleet. Accordingly CHARLIE FORCE (Captain F R D Pearce), comprising C Troop, an HW Section, sixteen tents, two LCVPs, to be manned' by LC Marines, two canoes, fourteen days rations and two units of fire (i.e. two outfits of ammunition) left as an advance party on 1 July 1951.

Wonsan Harbour is a large bay guarded by two peninsulas some five miles apart; Hodo Pando to the north and Kalmagak to the south. The bay is about ten miles deep. Inside and across the entrance of the bay are a number of islands, the largest and furthest east being Yo-Do. A large area within the bay had been swept clear of mines and here usually three destroyers circled to bombard opportunity targets. Occasionally communist batteries opened up, whereupon the destroyers and any other ships present would increase speed and return fire (called Operation WAR DANCE). When 41 Independent Commando arrived some of the islands were garrisoned by RoK Marines and a number of separate intelligence organisations were based on Yo-Do.

Through late summer and autumn, 41 Commando extended its operations by taking over various islands as patrol bases. B Troop (Captain E T G Shuldham) occupied Modo on 9 August. Later D Troop (Captain A Stoddart) took over Taedo, some 1,200 yards from Kalmagak, when the Leper colony there had been evacuated in November. After its RoK Marine garrison had been overwhelmed by a communist raid, Hwanto-Do was reoccupied by a force from D Troop led by Lieutenant J R H Walter and the garrison reinforced in December by Heavy Weapons whose 81mm mortars and 75mm recoilless rifle had already used this island for shoots against targets on the mainland. Defensive positions were dug on all islands to withstand return shell and mortar fire and beach exits were mined. SFCP and Heavy Weapons fire controllers frequently directed naval gunfire from OPs on occupied and unoccupied islands including Umi-Do 300 yards from a battery of 76mm anti-tank guns used against UN ships.

B and C Troop canoe patrols made six landings on Hodo Pando. During one of these Lieutenant Harwood and Sergeant Barnes of B Troop were killed in a patrol clash on 30 August. Also at this time B Troop's LCPR broke down off Modo and was driven ashore on Kalmagak. TSM Day and the four ranks with him were taken prisoner.

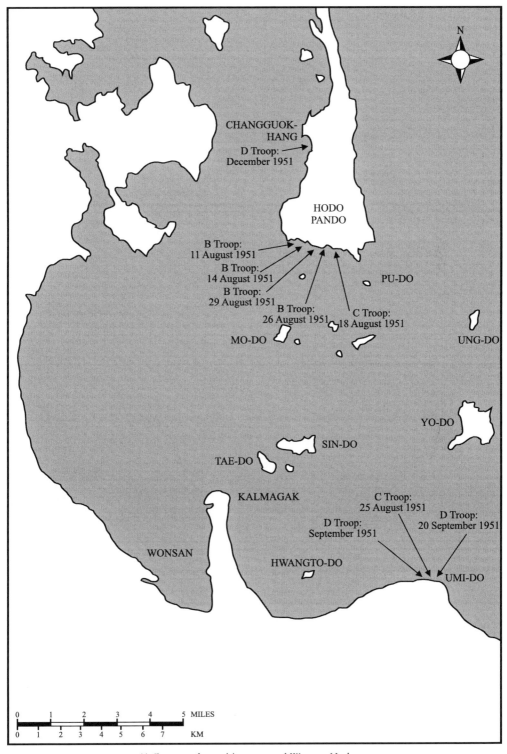

41 Commando positions around Wonsan Harbour

Captain Anthony 'Lofty' Stoddart RM

Lieutenant Tony Collin

Lieutenant John Harwood RM pictured during the Chosin phase

Lieutenant John Walter RM at Hagaru-ri

The graves of Lieutenant Harwood and Sergeant Barnes

On 27 September B Troop, accompanied by Lieutenant Colonel Drysdale, embarked in the USS *Wantuck* for a raid in the Songjin area the following night. The plan was for one party to secure a tunnel entrance to attract enemy reaction whilst a second party made a clandestine landing by canoes to ambush enemy reinforcements moving from Songjin. In the event the tunnel party was fired on and withdrew after one Marine was wounded. The ambush party laid mines on the road and as it was withdrawing heard the sound of trucks moving followed by an explosion. Both parties re-embarked by 0400 hours and returned to Modo in the afternoon on 29 September.

Lieutenant Colonel Douglas Drysdale RM in a landing craft off Modo

Yodo Jetty with Royal Marine manned LCVPs

On 3 October D Troop, reinforced by the Assault Engineers, UDT swimmers and a rocket launcher team from B Troop, all under command of the 2IC, embarked in USS *Wantuck* for operations south of Chongjin. After a night rehearsal on 4 October two parties totalling thirty-four attempted the following night to repeat the plan of the previous raid. However the UDT reconnaissance indicated that the railway was more heavily guarded than before and both parties withdrew,

On 6 October, ten men, preceded by two canoes led by Lieutenant J R H Walter attempted a landing a mile north of Sorye Dong but the first canoe came under fire as it beached and the force retired.

Corporal Maill and some of his section instructing members of the
Korean Marine Corps in the use of the 81mm mortar

43

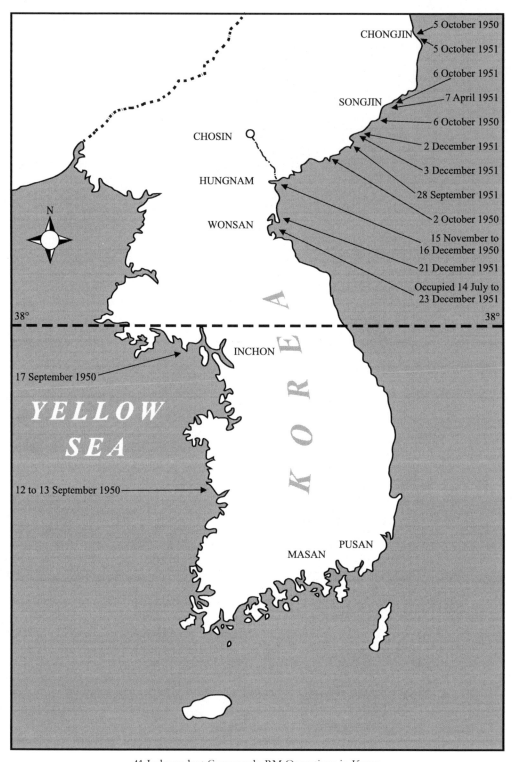

41 Independent Commando RM Operations in Korea

Lieutenant Colonel F N Grant relieved Lieutenant Colonel Drysdale on 15 October 1951 and moved up to the islands soon afterwards. On 30 November B Troop, accompanied by the Commanding Officer embarked in USS *Bass*. After a preliminary destroyer bombardment the Troop landed at 2300 hours on 2 December midway between Songjin and Hung Nam. Opposition was met on beaching and a Corporal and two Marines were wounded. The raiding party withdrew.

The following night B Troop made another landing one mile north of the previous night's target. (During the run in, a train was seen moving along the line). Opposition was again encountered and the force again withdrew after a Sergeant, Corporal and two Marines had been wounded by grenade fragments. The Commanding Officer, TSM Dodds and the UDT under Lieutenant Roman USN tried to plant some explosive to the north of the landing but a charge was dropped under the landing craft ramp. The craft got stuck and the party got clear just before the charge blew.

The force re-embarked and by 2100 hours on 4 December was back at Yo-Do.

Meanwhile, operations continued in Wonsan harbour: Desultory shelling, a typhoon and rescue of survivors from crashed aircraft. Rifle troops and HQ personnel were rotated through Sasebo. Tents were winterised and cold weather clothing issued in preparation for another winter in North Korea. Heavy seas made re-supply difficult.

At this stage the policy behind 41 Commando's raids was questioned. It was suggested the unit was wasting its time in Wonsan Harbour on defensive operations for which a Commando was inappropriate and that raids would become impracticable in winter.

In fact raids were carried out in the winter and more were planned in conjunction with some 800 RoK Marines who had been placed under Colonel Grant's command. These were not raids for raiding's sake but an effective means of tying down a quite disproportionate number of enemy forces who were forever conscious that a raid might be a prelude to a landing in strength by 1 Marine Division.

Colonel Grant had made some headway with the idea of 'keeping the coast alive' using rocky landing techniques on headlands instead of the heavily guarded beaches, when the totally unexpected order came in late December 1951 for 41 Independent Commando to withdraw. One final canoe raid called Operation SWANSONG was carried out by Lieutenant Walter and Sergeant Dodds of D Troop who destroyed enemy craft at Changguok Hang two miles up the west coast of Hodo Pando.

On 22/23 December 41 Independent Commando handed over to the RoK Marine Corps and embarked for Sasebo.

Chapter Seven

Disbandment and Conclusions

It was decided that those who had served less than a year overseas should complete their foreign tours in 3 Commando Brigade and the remainder of 41 Independent Commando RM should return to the UK. The unit embarked in the troopship SS *Empire Orwell* at Kure. The contingent destined for Malaya left at Singapore and the majority of the Commando continued to Southampton for an ecstatic welcome and a long train journey to Plymouth.

41 Independent Commando was formally disbanded on Stonehouse Barracks parade on 22 February 1952. The fortunate ones went on leave but thirty-one members of the unit had been left on Korean soil and it was not until mid-1954 that the last of the nineteen surviving Royal Marine prisoners of war were repatriated.

For the first time since the wars of religion, prisoners had been subjected to psychological 'interrogation' for ideological reasons: brainwashing. One Royal Marine elected to remain in China as the only British defector. Others showed great gallantry in resisting interrogation by all possible means. No one should condemn without themselves having experienced the four-year ordeal for which none of the United Nations Forces had at that time been prepared. Ten Royal Marines died in the grim conditions under which they were held (See Appendix G).

Hung Nam evacuation. Amtracks taking commandos to USS *General Randall*

What had 41 Independent Commando achieved in the eventful eighteen months of its existence? The unit had made some eighteen amphibious landings on the enemy coast. Eleven of these had been directed against one of the major communist supply routes and, as the later raids showed; considerable forces were diverted from the main battle area for its protection. The enemy attached great importance to Wonsan which was a focal point for the north/south and lateral road and rail traffic. 41 Commando's presence on the islands must have been a constant thorn in the communist flank.

Although so small a unit could make but little impact on the operations of the 1st US Marine Division at the Chosin Reservoir, the effect on the morale of the hard pressed US Marines, who were beginning to think they were 'the only troops fighting this goddamn war', was out of all proportion to the numbers involved. The comradeship and mutual respect engendered between the two Corps endures to this day.

New lessons were learned and many old ones relearned, about raiding techniques and the command and control of amphibious operations. For the next twenty years the Corps was primarily to be engaged on antiterrorist duties during the withdrawal from Empire. Many of those who served in 41 Independent Commando were to attain high commissioned and non-commissioned rank. Their operational experience became relevant to the Corp's present role in NATO.

41 Independent Commando made a small but significant contribution to the history of our Corps. This account is offered as a record of its activities and achievements and as a tribute to those who did not return.

Appendices

Notes on Weapons, Clothing and Equipment Used by 41 Independent Commando Royal Marines

Personal Weapons

Rifles

The rifleman was armed with the Ml Rifle (Garand) a semi-automatic .30 calibre weapon loaded with an eight round clip. Training was facilitated because latterly the wartime commandos had been armed with the Garand and a number of officers and NCOs were familiar with the mechanism.

Carbines

An early mistake was to issue too many of the superficially attractive Ml (and M3s which could fire bursts) lightweight carbines. These were soon discarded in the Chosin phase when even signallers were glad to carry Garands, as they were more reliable in the sub-zero temperatures and more effective against mass attacks, Both the Ml Rifle and Carbine had bayonets.

Submachine Guns (SMGs)

The official SMG was the M3 .45 calibre Submachine Carbine similar to a 9mm Sten gun. Nicknamed the Grease Gun because of its appearance, the weapon was not liked. Some old Thompson 1926 model Submachine Guns were acquired and became very sought after.

Pistols

The .45 Colt Automatic was the standard sidearm; another weapon familiar to the wartime commandos.

Grenades

Confidence was quickly lost in US fragmentation grenades which had many blinds (they were issued primed and it was believed they had been stored badly). Arrangements were therefore made for 36 grenades to be obtained, the only British weapons used by the Commando.

Crew Served Weapons

Light Machine Guns

Bren groups in rifle sections were equipped with Browning Automatic Rifles (BAR), which fired .30 calibre rifle ammunition from twenty round magazines. Although mounted on bipods it was probably expecting too much to use them to replace Bren Guns. The BAR became unreliable in sub-zero temperatures.

Medium Machine Guns (MMGs)

The Browning MMG belt fed mechanism was available on three models; an air cooled, bipod mounted LMG (A6) version with a booster cup which enabled it to fire 900rpm; a light tripod mounted air cooled (A4) version and the M1917(A1) water cooled version on a heavy tripod. Initially the Heavy Weapons sections were armed with the A4 but these proved incapable of sustained fire and after Chosin were replaced with the Al as being comparable to the Vickers The No 1 gun is in the Royal Marines Museum. Conversion of Heavy Weapons specialists from the Vickers to the Browning was straightforward. The former had seventeen stoppages to master. The Browning had four. There were also .5 Browning Heavy Machine Guns which were on the islands in Wonsan Harbour and used against targets on the mainland.

Mortars

Again beguiled by the lightweight weapons available, the 60mm mortar was first selected. This was a miniature 81mm mortar but required the same skills to fire a disappointingly small bomb a mere 2,000 yards. The 60mm mortar was given to the Rifle Troops to use without a tripod in a similar manner to the British two inch mortar and the Heavy Weapons took over the 81mm mortars which proved far more effective than the three inch mortar they had been trained upon. It was accurate, fired light and heavy HE and two types of smoke bombs and, with supercharge, could reach out to 4,500 yards. (At that time the British three inch mortar's maximum range was 2,800 yards).

Mils

Compasses, mortar sights and machine gun tripods were graduated in mils. A mil is defined as the angle subtended by 1 unit at 1,000 units and, although a very useful fire control measurement, training was necessary to convert all ranks from degrees (360° to the circle) to mils (6,440 to the circle). This training was very useful in later years when the British adopted the mils measurement.

Anti Tank Weapons

Although the Commando encountered no tank threat, 2.65 inch rocket launchers (the original bazooka) and later the 3.5 inch, which became the standard British platoon anti tank weapon were available. On the islands the Heavy Weapons group acquired a 75mm Recoilless Rifle which was fired with some effect against targets on the mainland.

Naval Gunfire and Air Support

The USMC had developed the close support of Naval gunfire, and Navy and Marine air wings, to a fine art during the Pacific Campaign. 41 Independent Commando had a shore fire control party (SFCP) permanently attached. Members of 41 Commando cannot speak too highly of the splendid support given by USMC and Navy pilots during the Chosin Reservoir campaign.

Radios

The US radios were generally a generation ahead of the British equivalent. The troop net radio was the short range SCR 536, in appearance like a large handset with a pull-out aerial. The Commando net set was the SCR 300 which was later adopted as the British 31 set. The ANG/RC 9 (or 'angry 9' as it was dubbed) provided longer range communications. A characteristic was its ability to be powered by hand cranking.

Cold Weather Clothing

During the Chosin Reservoir phase when the Commando was operating in snow and ice, with a high wind-chill factor and night temperatures down to 56°F of frost, the average marine was dressed in the following layers of clothing:

1. Normal underwear
2. Longjohns and string vest
3. Angola shirt, or US equivalent
4. One or more woollen jerseys
5. Battledress top and trousers (or US equivalent)
6. Combat jacket and trousers
7. Pile-lined parka with hood (a USMC parka as worn in 41 Commando is displayed in the Royal Marines Museum)

The Green Beret was worn under the parka hoods. On the hands were worn either ski mitts with a woollen inner or, more usefully, woollen gloves with leather outers. The least satisfactory item was the footwear: shoepacks. These were rubber and gutta-percha calf length lace-up boots with felt insoles. Intended for cold, wet conditions they were cumbersome and slippery and caused many cases of frostbite because the sweat could not be absorbed. To quote the USMC history:

> 'In the cumbersome shoepacks perspiration soaked feet gradually became transformed into lumps of biting pain… When men are immobilised for hours in such temperatures, no amount of clothing will keep them warm. Yet, even more disturbing was the effect of the weather on carbines and BARs. These weapons froze to such a degree that they became unreliable or completely unserviceable. The M-l rifle and the Browning machine guns showed stubborn streaks but retained their effectiveness, provided they were cared for properly.'

Unit Lanyards

The 'buttons and bows' buffs might be interested to learn the origin of 41 Commando's yellow lanyard. On arrival in Japan the only lanyards available were the white sailor's lanyards from Naval Stores. These were soaked in a solution of the anti-malarial drug Mepacrine; the only dye available, (Yellow had been the colour of 5 Army Commando of 3 Commando Brigade).

Cold Weather Clothing

Raiding Techniques

Apart from the Sorye Dong raid on 7 April 1951, all 41 Independent Commando's raids were clandestine operations conducted at night and were in two troop strength or less. The close approach was made in rubber boats, later augmented by SBS type two man canoes. The US LCR(L) (Landing Craft Rubber – Large) carried ten men (Coxswain, bowman and eight paddlers) and up to 400 pounds of explosives in ten pound packs.

Parent ships (usually Assault Personnel Destroyers – APDs) were under orders not to cross the 100 fathom line because of the moored mine threat and although they frequently closed to seventy fathoms to support the commandos this still meant about an eight-mile run in.

An LCPR at Modo

As the APDs closed the coast dim red lights would be switched on in the troop spaces to aid night acclimatisation. On 'Action Stations' being sounded troops would fall in at their boat stations. The four LCPRs (Landing Craft Personnel – Ramped) would be lowered; troops would inflate their LCR(L)s, pass them down into the Landing Craft and thence outboard into the water. Each Rifle Section would embark across the Landing Craft and the explosives would be handed down and stowed. As

An assault engineer linking a 'beehive' charge during the Sorye Dong raid

each LCR(L) was loaded it would hook on to the tow rope and stream astern of its landing craft in the one knot way maintained by the APD. When all was complete, with five or six rubber boats to each craft, the long tow in to the beach would begin. The LCVPs, moving at three or four knots, would be vectored in by the APD following their progress on radar and passing course corrections over the radio.

About 1,000 yards off the beach the rubber boats would slip their tows and stand off while the reconnaissance boat, or canoe, closed the beach, sending swimmers in if necessary to check the surf and beach defences. Then the covering force would land, clear the beach area and deploy to form a defensive perimeter around the objective.

Next to land would be the demolition and humping parties organised by the Beachmaster. The Assault Engineers would lay the charges which would take up to four hours. Each ten pound pack had to be carefully laid and connected in a ringmain with Cordtex so all detonated simultaneously. There had to be at least two methods of initiation and customarily several time clocks were used with a twenty to forty minute setting.

When the AEs were ready to withdraw, fuses were pulled and orders given to withdraw. The force would thin out, return to the beach and re-embark under the directions of the Beachmaster. Rubber boats would be launched and paddled out (lighter now) through the surf to pick up their tows. The waiting LCPR (which could have beached in emergency to recover casualties or prisoners) would then begin the long haul back to the waiting APDs. As they cleared the area the charges would detonate giving a feeling of immense satisfaction at a job well done. Alongside, the rubber boats would be recovered, deflated, weapons inspected and troops would go below. Even though officially dry the USN would generously break out the medical brandy to help celebrate a successful operation.

*

Appendix C

Organisation of 41 Independent Commando

In the 1950s the Royal Marines Commandos were organised as in the Second World War with five Rifle Troops, a Heavy Weapons Troop and a Headquarters Troop. (The Company organisation was not introduced until 1962). The Rifle Troop was some sixty strong, commanded by a Captain, with a small Troop HQ including two unattached subalterns and four large Rifle Sections commanded by Sergeants.

41 Independent Commando RM was a much smaller organisation. At most it consisted of 300 of all ranks and fluctuated according to casualties and the availability of reinforcements. During the early raids only Signallers and Assault Engineers were used in their specialist roles. All other trades and specialisations were employed as riflemen.

The Unit was organised on an ad hoc basis, as groups arrived and men were trained on US weapons and raiding techniques, initially comprising three small Troops, or Patrols, one each embarked in the USS *Perch*, *Bass* and *Wantuck*. Before joining the 1st Marine Division the Commando was formally organised into three Rifle Troops each about forty-five strong. The Heavy Weapons Group and the Assault Engineers were part of Commando Headquarters.

A note on the organisation of the Heavy Weapons Group might illustrate the flexibility of the organisation. The standard mortar or machine gun section consists of two detachments of three men each. In 41 Independent Commando the versatility of Royal Marines' dual training was exploited by having two sections each of two four man detachments. In defence, as in Wonsan Harbour deployed in support of the island garrisons, the Group could man all four mortars and four machine guns (with a 75mm recoilless rifle as well on Hwanto-Do) with two crew to each weapon. Permutations with fewer guns or mortars were necessary for more mobile operations when larger detachments were required.

Captain Edward T G Shuldham RM briefs members of B Troop, 41 Independent Commando RM prior to a daylight raid against enemy supply routes eight miles south of Songjint North Korea

Command, Administration and Morale

41 Commando's independence meant that without the support of a Brigade, or other British Headquarters, very much more responsibility devolved on the Commanding Officer. Not only was he involved with operational planning but he had to obtain logistic support from an ally and personnel matters had to be referred to the Royal Marines Office in London. Examples of some of the problems and how they were overcome follow.

Command

To release the Commanding Officer for planning operations with the Staff of Commander US 7th Fleet and his Task Group Commanders, the Commanding Officier delegated much of the responsibility for the internal administration of the Unit to his Second-in-Command; Major D L S St M Aldridge. Thus the Unit was commissioned HMS *41 Commando* with the Second-in-Command becoming Executive Officer and having powers under the Naval Discipline Act. Offenders could be awarded ninety days detention to start from arrival in HMS *Tamar* in Hong Kong. In the event use was made of suspended sentences which did not deprive the much under-strength Unit of the services of the infrequent offenders.

Dollars

41 Commando was despatched to live and work with United States forces without arranging for the officers and men to be paid in dollars. For some weeks this caused very real embarrassment, The British Armed Forces currency (BAFs) issued to Commonwealth occupation forces in Japan was unacceptable in Camp McGill's messes, canteens and the PX. The Ambassador and his Staff at the British Embassy in Tokyo could not have been more helpful to the Commanding Officer (indeed on return from the Chosin Reservoir action the whole Commando was invited to the Embassy) and the Naval Attaché, Commander 'Jock' Gray emptied his safe of dollars to enable Lieutenant Colonel Drysdale to pay the Unit. Later all pay was made in dollars plus a handsome allowance of four dollars a day to officers and one dollar daily to other ranks.

Reinforcements

Without the support of a reinforcement holding unit there were long delays before casualties were replaced, particularly after Chosin when 41 Independent Commando became non operat¬ional because of severe shortages in specialist categories (signallers, heavy weapons and assault engineers). 3 Commando Brigade, which was heavily engaged in winning the antiterrorist campaign in Malaya, was unable to spare reinforcements until later, when a welcome draft of experienced NCOs and marines volunteered to join 41 Commando instead of being repatriated.

Once reinforcements arrived in theatre a further ten days training was required on US weapons and raiding techniques (Appendices A and B) before they were available for operations.

Chaplain

41 Commando was not large enough to rate a Chaplain but the absence of one when operating with foreign forces was particularly felt, not only to conduct burial services but once the unit started to suffer casualties many would have appreciated regular services and the welfare support of a Naval Chaplain. The Billy Graham Evangelical Campaign book did not have the reassuring familiarity of the Book of Common Prayer.

Administrative Command

On returning to Japan from Chosin, General Sir Horace Robertson, the Australian Commander of the British Commonwealth Forces there, demanded to assume administrative command of 41 Independent Commando and the unit was 'banished' from Ebisu Camp, Tokyo to HMAS *Commonwealth* at Kure where the men were accommodated in considerable discomfort in the cinema to satisfy his megalomania. It is significant that from the moment the Commando was removed from US logistic support the British Government had to pay in hard won dollars for all its US supplied clothing and equipment.

Later the Commando's rear echelon was based on an old Japanese seaplane station near HMS *Ladybird* at Sasebo from where British supplies could be drawn for those not on active service in Wonsan Harbour.

Leadership and Morale

41 Independent Commando was a very young unit, the Commanding Officer was only thirty-four at the time of the Chosin Reservoir action, but the intensely high morale which applied throughout, apart from a short period after being withdrawn from 1 Marine Division, stemmed from Lieutenant Colonel Drysdale's inspired leadership augmented by a high proportion of wartime experienced officers and NCOs. The high standards of individual training provided by the Corps also helped greatly.

The spirit of the Unit is exemplified by a number of 'characters':

Second Lieutenant George Mann

 The Quartermaster. Formerly the Corps QMSI of PT George Mann had recently been commissioned and 41 Commando was his first appointment. Mercifully he had not been indoctrinated with standard stores accounting procedures and instead used his resource, initiative and not a little charm to acquire the necessities and some luxuries from our generous American allies. Being older than other subalterns the Americans frequently mistook his one 'pip' for a Brigadier General's insignia. George tended not to disabuse them of the mistake.

RSM Jimmy Baines

'Sticks' Baines, as he was known to many, was promoted direct from his substantive rank of Colour Sergeant for distinguished service in the field whilst serving with 41 Independent Commando. As RSM he was a strict disciplinarian and set a fine personal example of courage and integrity. One sometimes despaired of ever measuring up to his seemingly impossible high standards yet he always had a sardonic twinkle in his eye. Jimmy Baines was the rock around which the Unit was anchored.

Corporal Dave Brady

Corporal Brady was one of the ubiquitous and ever useful Assault Engineers. He was also the unit wag, ready with a joke or wisecrack at appropriate – and often inappropriate – times. Once in a cinema crowded with Royal and US Marines the film broke and Dave Brady took the stage. The audience preferred Brady when the film had been repaired; and it wasn't a bad film.

*

There were others who in their own way contributed to the splendid team which was 41 Independent Commando including Corporal Don Sauncheqrow, the United States Marine Driver of the Heavy Weapons 30 cwt truck temporarily attached for the drive from Hung Nam to Hagaru-ri. Not only did he drive the last truck into the beleaguered perimeter laden with wounded but he declined to rejoin his parent unit and he and 'old faithful' stayed with the Commando as its only organic load carrying transport. During the withdrawal the truck slid off the road and was demolished. Don Saunchegrow marched out with his Royal Marines comrades and still keeps in touch. This 'honorary Royal Marine' was flown to the twentieth reunion of 41 Independent Commando on the orders of the Commandant of the Marine Corps.

*

Note: Colonel Drysdale died on 22 June 1990 three weeks after attending a reunion of seventy-two members of his former command including representatives of G Company and the USMC tank battalion from Force DRYSDALE. It is a measure of the esteem in which he was held that twenty-four former members of 41 Independent Commando Royal Marines attended the funeral which was held in the remote Norfolk village of East Bradenham.

Major General F N Grant CB died on 9 September 1991

Seventy-three Korean war veterans met at Bickleigh for the 25th anniversary reunion on 29 November 1975. Pictured here in the front line (left to right): Captain George Mann, RSM Jimmy Baines MM BEM, Colonel Douglas Drysdale DSO OBE and Major General Pat Ovens CB OBE MC

Roll of Honour
Killed in Action, Died of Wounds or in Captivity

Captain R N Parkinson-Cumine MC RM

Surgeon Lieutenant D A Knock MB BS RN

Lieutenant J G Harwood RM

Sergeant C E Barnes RM

Acting Petty Officer J A Tate RN

Acting Sergeant R G Davies RM

Corporal P B Babb RM

Corporal J E Belsey RM

Corporal C R B Hill RM

Corporal Ronald Southworth RM

Corporal C E Trott RM

L/SBA Dennis Raines RN

Marine Gerard Aherne

Marine A J Aldrich

Marine Evan Garner

Marine J L Graham

Marine L A Heard

Marine S E H Hills

Marine K D Hitchman

Marine W L J Jauncey

Marine P R Jones

Marine Harry Melling

Marine Joseph McCourt

Marine R J Needs

Marine Reuben Nichols

Marine Stanley Skelton

Marine Eric Strain

Marine D W Stray

Marine W A Walker

Marine Royston Wooldridge

Marine Kenneth Wyeth

Honours and Awards
Ranks and decorations given are those at the time the awards were promulgated

British Decorations

Distinguished Service Order
Major (Acting Lieutenant Colonel) D B Drysdale MBE RM
Captain E T G Shuldham RM

Distinguished Service Cross
Lieutenant J R H Walter RM

Military Cross
Captain D L St M Aldridge MBE RM
Captain L G Marsh RM
Captain P J Ovens RM

Distinguished Service Medal
QMS R R Dodds RM
SBA (Acting LSBA) Evan Critchley

Military Medal
Colour Sergeant (Acting QMS) J Baines BEM
Marine G Bramble
Corporal E Cruse
Marine A A H Harper
Marine M Hine
Sergeant R W D James
Corporal H Langton
Corporal G Maindonald
Marine R Twigg

Mention in Despatches
Sergeant C E Barnes

Lieutenant G F D Roberts RM
Surgeon Lieutenant D A Knock MB BS RN (Posthumous)
Act Petty Officer J A Tate (Posthumous)
Leading Seaman A J Futcher
Lieutenant P R Thomas RM
Sergeant W M Mackay
Corporal D A Torr
Marine F Roberts
Marine S Vardy

Queen's Commendation
QMS J Day

Admiralty Commendation
Marine S Hicks
Marine PD Murphy

United States Decorations

Silver Star
Major (Acting Lieutenant Colonel) D B Drysdale DSO MBE RM (Two Silver Stars)
Captain (Local Major) D L St M Aldridge MBE MC RM

Legion of Merit
Major F N Grant RM

Bronze Star with Combat V
RSM J Baines MM BEM RM
Corporal R Baker
QMS F C Hambleton
Marine A J Lansdowne
Sergeant J J Maill
Sergeant S J Moon
Captain E G D Pounds RM
Lieutenant G F D Roberts RM
Captain P R Thomas RM
Sergeant J Whiting

Presidential Unit Citation
41 Independent Commando Royal Marines

Altar set (later stolen) presented to Bickleigh Parish Church in memory of those who died in 41
Independent Commando RM

Prisoners of War

QMS J Day

Acting Sergeant R G Davies*

Corporal F Beadle

Corporal E Curd

Corporal C R B Hill*

Corporal W Peskett

Corporal G R Richards

Corporal D R Treagus

Marine G Ahern*

Marine A J Aldrich*

Marine G F Balchin

Marine P Banfield

Marine W E Brown

Marine A M Condron

Marine W G Cox

Marine T Darby

Marine J E Goodman

Marine L A Heard*

Marine S Hicks

Marine S E H Hills*

Marine B Martin

Marine C McKee

Marine H Melling*

Marine P D Murphy

Marine R J Needs*

Marine R Nichols*

Marine R Ogle

Marine J Underwood

Marine K Wyeth*

[*Died in Captivity]

QMS Day disembarking from HMT *Dunera* at Southampton on 16 October 1953

Twenty nine members of 41 Independent Commando were captured by communist forces, twenty-four from the convoy when the rear of the Commando was cut off. They fought through the night of 28/29 November with members of the Divisional Train and the US Army Company under the command of Major McLaughlin USMC who reluctantly decided to surrender due to mounting casualties and shortage of ammunition. These unfortunate individuals thus endured five months more incarceration for instance than those captured after the Imjin River battle. Five more were captured in September 1951 when their landing craft broke down in Wonsan Harbour. After initial capture POWs were subjected to forced marches without treatment for wounds or all-pervasive dysentery. Particularly brutal were the North Korean guards running 'Paks Palace', infamous for its high death rate and 'Tiger', the viciously sadistic commander of a column of prisoners comprising civilian internees and UN Forces. Of the original 850, only 265 survived their long captivity. One Royal Marine in this column was G Ahern who was befriended by a US Soldier, Shorty Estabrook. He wrote afterwards:

> 'Gerry Ahern, the only British soldier amongst us, died in my arms. He had been machine-gunned, both his legs and feet were riddled with bullet holes. Without any medical attention Jerry was a doomed man. He died like a man, far away from his beloved England. He was amongst friends and we loved him like a brother.'

Throughout his captivity and long afterwards Shorty cherished the Green Beret worn by Marine Ahem.

Such were the harsh conditions under which 41 Commando prisoners were held that ten died in captivity and not since the Wars of Religion have prisoners been subjected to psychological interrogation for ideological reasons or 'brain washing'. This comprised attendance at compulsory lectures lasting several hours even when conditions were freezing. No one should condemn without having themselves experienced the three-year ordeal for which none of the United Nations Forces at that time had been prepared. Indeed many showed great gallantry in resisting interrogation by all possible means. QMS Day was awarded a Queens's Commendation for Brave Conduct and Marine Stan Hicks and Marine P D Murphy were awarded Admiralty Commendations for Exemplary Conduct as POWs.

During the long and tedious peace talks at Panmunjon, repatriation of Prisoners of War continued to be a serious obstacle. A breakthrough was made in April 1953 when some sick and wounded prisoners were exchanged. On 27 July 1953 an end to fighting was agreed and a system for prisoner repatriation was approved. Those not wishing to return to their own country would be handed over to representatives of neutral nations. Thousands of North Koreans and Chinese decided not to return but of 75,000 Prisoners of War taken by the communists 62,000 had perished. When the communists realised the importance of Prisoners of War, conditions in their camps started to improve. Members of 41 Commando had been housed in different camps. When released they were reunited in Kure, Japan where they were interrogated over their part in the conflict and experiences as a Prisoner of War. They found it hurtful being asked stupid questions by young officers who had no experience of soldiering and gave the impression that all former prisoners were suspected of being communists. They found this attitude persisted when they had returned to the UK where after four years away they were only met by a Non-commissioned Officer from the Pay and Records Office who issued them with a Leave Pass, Rail Warrant and a Ration Book. The only person to acknowledge their release from some three years as Prisoners of War was Colonel Drysdale, by that time serving at the US Marine Corps Schools, Quantico. He wrote this example on 12 August 1953:

Dear Marine Underwood,

I wish I could be at home to greet you in person, but as circumstances will not allow this, I am writing you the short note of welcome instead.

No-one who was not there can have a full understanding of the boredom, the frustration and hardships under which you must have suffered during your long captivity. However I can imagine there must have been times when you thought it would never come to an end and that you were doomed to become forgotten men. Believe me; those in 41 Commando never forgot you. You were constantly in our thoughts. The unit made a great name for itself and in the building of that reputation you played your full part.

Now that you have returned home I hope that first you enjoy some very hardly and well-earned leave with your families and get a job that you will like.

If ever, and I say this with the deepest sincerity, there is anything that I can do to help you in any way, please drop me a line at the above address (at Quantico) where I expect to be until February. After that I can always be contacted through the RMO or through Mr Webb at the Royal Marines Association, 5 Talbot Square, London.

Yours Sincerely

D B Drysdale

A number of former Prisoners of War spent much of their leave in hospital. Their condition deteriorated and they became unfit for further service. It was well into 1954 before those considered fit returned to duty. Those who did continue in the Corps were so disenchanted with their reception that none re-engaged for further service after their engagements had expired.

A photograph released by the *China News Agency* showing Royal Marines captured after the convoy battle on 29/30 November 1950. In front is Marine Harry Melling, who died in captivity.

One who did not return was Marine Andrew Condron, the only Briton to remain of the 327 UN Personnel who decided to stay with the communists. This was agreed by the British representative at the Cease Fire talks. The majority of British newspapers denounced him as a traitor and collaborator. Some proclaimed he was afraid of reprisals from fellow prisoners. All this came from journalists who had never met the man and was reiterated by some former Prisoners of War who had not been in the same camp as Condron. Those who had firmly refute the allegation. John Underwood wrote:

> 'Andrew Condron never betrayed anyone nor was he guilty of collaboration. His only sin was that he was able to improve the lot of many Prisoners of War because he constantly pressurised the Chinese. For that I am thankful.'

A member of the 8th Hussars wrote:

> 'Those of us who knew Andy in Camp Five had, and still have, the very highest regard for him and there is no doubt that he did more for the British Prisoners of War than the next twenty of us put together. He was very often with the Chinese when the rest of us were doing our daily skylarking and he did his share of dirty jobs. He was beaten up on interrogation sessions, which did not occur with the majority.'

Condron was discharged SNLR –Service No Longer Required – not as a deserter. In Peking he and the twenty-one Americans who stayed were treated as honoured guests. Mr and Mrs Winnington of the *Daily Worker* looked after him and he attended Peking University. He married the French/Chinese daughter of a French diplomat in 1959. At the start of the Cultural Revolution the Chinese had no further use for him and he returned the UK in October 1962. In 1968 he attended a 41 Independent Commando reunion at CTCRM. Colonel Drysdale stopped any resentment at his presence but one member upset by his presence wrote him a bitter letter afterwards. He received a polite and reasoned response to which he replied apologising unreservedly. Andrew Condron died on 12 March 1986.

Acknowledgement is made to former Colour Sergeant Hayhurst's book *Green Berets in Korea*, published by Vanguard Press for much of the information contained in this Appendix.

Royal Marine Cruiser Detachments
in the Korean War
A *Sheet Anchor* Article by Lieutenant Colonel Peter Thomas

The exploits of 41 Independent Commando Royal Marines in the Korean War are well documented, but little publicity has hitherto been given to the activities of the RM Ships' detachments during this conflict.

*

All naval operations during the Korean War were under the command of the US 7th Fleet. The Commonwealth naval forces operated mainly on the west coast which was characterised as having an up to ten metre tidal range with many drying creeks and islands and fierce tidal streams. The Royal Navy maintained two cruisers on station throughout the war all of which had Royal Marines detachments.

HMS *Ceylon*

The first was HMS *Ceylon*, which brought the Argyll and Sutherland Highlanders up from Hong Kong (the Middlesex Regiment was lifted in the aircraft carrier HMS *Unicorn*). Initially the *Ceylon*'s detachment was reinforced to two platoon strength. On 20 May 1951 it had landed under the OCRM, Captain Kelsey-Burge, with

Lieutenant N S E Martin, relieved by Lieutenant J D Hunter, in craft provided by the USS *Colmstock*, on Choda Island, then penetrated one and a half miles inland and set fire to two villages. This was on information from the 'Leopard' organisation which cooperated with Anti-Communist North Korean guerrillas. Other cruisers were the *Belfast*, *Birmingham*, *Jamaica*, *Kenya* and *Newcastle*.

Newcastle's Sergeant Major Forster recorded the whole two year deployment in the Detachment diary, which incidentally informs us that during a year in Korean waters she fired 1,552 x 6" shells, 1,242 x 4" and 4,419 x 40mm. Although most cruiser detachments made landings, those by the Ceylon were the most costly as described by two of the Royal Marines engaged.

HMS Ceylon's Raid – Sogon Ni, by Marine C F Self, 24/25 August 1951

'It was planned that during the day we would rendezvous with the New Zealand frigate HMNZS *Rotoiti* and we, the landing party, would make the landing from her during the night. She could get closer inland than the *Ceylon* and the run-in would be made using the two small motor boats carried by the *Rotoiti*. We then heard that a few of the New Zealand sailors wanted to come with us and I think three volunteered. I don't know whether Lieutenant Hunter, the replacement officer, agreed but nothing more was said and we were able to get our heads down for a few hours.

'After a snack at 2300 hours we mustered on the quarterdeck, primed our grenades and had a look at the map of the area which showed where we would land, where the target was supposed to be and were told the signals to be used. So we were ready as ever we would be. This time I actually volunteered to be in the snatching party with the Lieutenant, a Corporal, four or five Marines and two or three of the sailors. The remaining Marines and some Sailors would hold the beachhead until we returned. At the most we were fifteen to twenty men.

'It was about 2330 hours and we clambered into the two small boats alongside. It was very dark indeed and very cramped as we headed for the shore which we couldn't see. The sound of the engines chugging away was very loud, no doubt magnified by the fact we were trying not to make a noise. It was about half an hour before we realised we were very close. The other boat arrived a little before us and had quietly disembarked. We had problems as we hit something under the water and had to back off several times before we finally got ashore waist deep in water.

'My section was waiting for me and we had a little roll-call on the beach. The boats backed off and as the beach party organized themselves we prepared to head off up the small cliff and as planned attempt to get a prisoner. We were now on dangerous ground unable to see as it was so dark as we clambered up this high sandy bank where we were to go off left at the top and make our way towards some slit trenches. Halfway up this bank we saw a sentry across to our right silhouetted against the night sky. We froze and waited till he had disappeared. So on we went crawling on our stomachs, stopping and starting and sweating mad with tension and the heat. It seemed ages crawling along this cliff top wondering how and when we would find the target. At this point the Lieutenant ordered the Corporal and two men off to the right to cover us and they scuttled away quietly. We gave them time to get in position, a good five minutes which seemed like a good five hours.

'Things were very tense as we moved forward again silently like snakes and I could sense the man behind me was close by my ankles. Suddenly there was a shout from right in front of us and only yards away. It was a challenge in a foreign sounding voice and a half-inch heavy machine gun opened fire right at us, my head hit the deck and I lifted my eyes and saw the tracer was passing just over my head a foot off the ground. I rolled to one side and was about to fire back as I could see exactly where it was coming from. At that moment something heavy fell across my boots. Then someone threw a grenade and the machine gun stopped. The grenade must have been thrown by one of the seamen as it took seven seconds explode (The Navy uses hand grenades with seven second fuses to throw over the sides of ships in harbour to deter divers from attaching explosives. We use only four second fuses in the land forces). During this surprise and short lull I heard the man behind me moan and the Lieutenant rolled across to me. I said to him that I thought the chap behind me had been hit. I later found out he had been hit in the stomach area and realised he had been crawling on his hands and knees. The Lieutenant told me we would have to abandon our intention and get this man back. He ordered me to stay where I was and cover him while he and one of the others in the party dragged this wounded man back to the edge of the cliff. I said "OK" and, visualising me on my own trying to hold out with just my rifle to fire back, I asked him to let me have his Sten Gun and gave him my Rifle. Then a long wait as they pulled and tugged with this heavy man across to the edge and down the cliff.

'It seemed like hours and I had no idea how long to wait but I did wait and then waited some more to make absolutely sure. Then I rolled slowly to the edge and listened. The Lieutenant came across and ordered me back up the cliff to try and get the Corporal and two men back. Well, I pulled myself back up to the top and peered over the edge, I was really knackered by this time and I couldn't see or hear anything so I decided I would pop my head up again and shout the Corporal's name. I shouted "McGregor" and bobbed down again and nothing happened. I thought I should try again and as I put my head over the top the second time there was a rush of feet coming straight at me. As I aimed the Sten Gun the thought came in my mind that if this wasn't the Corporal I shall have to open fire, luckily I waited right till the last second and saw silhouetted McGregor and two men. I told him we were getting out and we all clambered down the cliff where we were told that the wounded man was dead. I was told to carry this poor unfortunate seaman and so with a little help to get him on my back I made the effort but he was too heavy for me and I was completely exhausted so two others carried him and

I brought up the rear as we plodded along this dark beach back to the landing area. It was slow and hard going and rocky underfoot and we were now hearing noises above us so we had to keep going, then the Very lights went up away ahead of us, the signal to retire. We reached a headland and it was pretty steep and an awful decision had to be made as time was really running out, it was decided by the Lieutenant to leave the seaman. It would have been almost impossible to get him and us out into the water and round this headland. His dog tags were removed and he was propped up against the rocks and I can remember how very sad I was to have to leave him. To this day I can visualize him.

'We scrambled out into the water and round these huge rocks with the waves splashing against them and it was some distance before we were able to see the boats on the beach waiting on tenterhooks for us to appear. It seemed there was some action up on the cliffs and the boats would have left without us if we hadn't appeared when we did. We clambered in and as we left we saw some men at the top of the cliff and opened fire just to keep their heads down while we negotiated the underwater rocks to get away. Back to the *Rotoiti* and glasses of rum all round but also a tot of sadness.

We returned to our own ship the *Ceylon* and were debriefed by the Captain of Marines. The following morning we went back to the *Rotoiti* for a Service on the Quarterdeck for AB Marchioni. It was extremely sad and the tears ran down my face quite unexpectedly.'

HMS Ceylon's Landing – Chomdong near Mongumpo, Choppeki Point, 30 August 1951

'Just five days later I was on another day out on the beach on a similar type of operation, so there I was along with about thirty other Marines with Lieutenant Hunter and a couple of sergeants etc in a landing craft early morning sun shining and we were heading for this lovely sandy looking beach with what looked like some sort of hut tucked in at the left hand side.

'The run-in was pretty smooth and the ramp went down and out we shot up the beach spreading out as we went. About a hundred yards up something hit my right thigh it felt like someone hitting me with a big lump of wood, I never heard a sound and over I went on to my face, after a few seconds I turned to my left and saw 'Butch' (the Marine butcher) and I realized I couldn't see out of my left eye, it had suddenly gone opaque. I said to Butch "Is my left eye still there?" He said "Yes" and I noticed he had been wounded in the right shoulder. Then I heard shouting from one of the sergeants standing by the landing craft and everyone was being dragged or running back into the landing craft. We must have set off quite a number of trip wire anti-personnel mines and almost everyone had been wounded in some way, so in just a few seconds the whole thing was over.

HMS *Ceylon* Y Turret Crew, 1951 – Lieutenant J D Hunter RM is on the second row five from the left

'I stood up and started to walk back down the beach with the Sergeant yelling his head off for me to hurry up but I collapsed and couldn't stand up. So I dragged myself along and got into the landing craft which was covered in blood. I saw one of my mates (Marine McKiernan) with half his leg exposed (he eventually lost it) and another one of my close mates lost a toe. It was then I discovered I had been hit in both shoulders and could hardly hold my arms up. Lieutenant Hunter, who had lead the landing, had a piece of shrapnel right up his backside, so in a few short seconds nineteen of the Platoon had been rendered useless and it could have been avoided because I heard later that it had been known about the beach being mined through Intelligence.

'I was hoisted up to the ship in a Neil Robinson stretcher, taken to the Sick bay, given first aid and an injection and I lay there wondering, *what next?* The sick bay filled up and the Surgeon Commander started to operate. I fell asleep it was night time when I awoke and the Surgeon had been working non-stop for hours fortified by a drink or two (he was a notorious drinker) and I suppose he hadn't been called on to actually do his duty as a Surgeon for years. Later on it was my turn for the Table and I can remember being given an injection and then oblivion, the shrapnel was removed from my leg and some from both shoulders, my eye was just bandaged up. It was then as I came round that I could feel the ship was making some speed; we were heading back for Sasebo in Japan and arrived next day. It wasn't long before I was passed over the side again into a ship's boat and headed towards the British Hospital Ship *Maine* where I and some of the others would receive better attention. I found myself on this hospital ship with just what I stood up in as I had to leave all my personal things on the *Ceylon* and I never saw any of it again, which was a shame because I had some souvenirs I would have liked to have taken home.

'From the hospital ship I alone was taken to an Army hospital to see a specialist about my eye. The specialist was a Major Jagger RAMC, who carried out a close inspection. He then took me to a room where inside was a huge magnet which was lowered over my eye and switched on. It didn't do anything for me. Major Jagger said that whatever it was still in my eye wasn't metal and he assumed it must be plastic and that it would disperse very slowly. As I write this it is fifty-nine years on and is still dispersing so he wasn't wrong."

The above are from an account written by former Royal Marine Cecil Self with details supplied by Marine Brian Harrison.

The official account of the raid may be found in BR 1736(54) – *Naval Staff History, British Commonwealth Naval Operations, Korea 1950–53*, Published 1967:

'A somewhat unfortunate raid was carried out early on 30 August. Its object was to round up a number of enemy troops reported by 'Leopard' to be in Chomdong (38 degrees 11' 10" N, 124 degrees 46 50" E). No serious opposition was expected but the raid was on a larger scale than heretofore, the landing party consisting of two platoons of Royal Marines and one of stoker-mechanics from HMS *Ceylon*. The assault party, Headquarters and one Marine platoon, under Captain H E Kelsey-Burge was to be followed ashore by the two remaining platoons if the beach-head was established.

'HM Ships *Ceylon* and *Concord* and HMNZS *Rotoiti* approached in the darkness to between one and two miles from the beach, and as soon as it was light enough for daylight spotting, delivered a heavy twelve-minute bombardment, while the assault party accompanied by Lieutenant Colonel Ergott USA proceeded ashore in an LCVP previously embarked at Sasebo (and manned by sailors from the *Ceylon*). The bombardment was then lifted inshore and the party landed. As they deployed across the beach, an accurate and heavy small arms fire opened from the flanks. The fire was returned, and covering bombardment was renewed while the party withdrew and re-embarked, but fifteen casualties, one of them serious, were suffered. Except for the coolness of Captain Burge and all concerned including the LCVP crew, the losses would have been heavier… There could be no doubt that the information of the intended raid had leaked out, and Admiral Scott-Moncrieff ordered such activities to be discontinued in future unless CTE 95.12 could be certain he was not being double-crossed.'

Those involved state that there was little or no small arms fire and that most of the wounds were caused by mortar fire and mines as would be confirmed by Marine Self's embedded plastic. The OCRM and the US Army officer were not with the first wave and were probably with the follow up platoon. Subsequently Captain H E K Burge RM was awarded the Distinguished Service Cross and Lieutenant (later Major) J D F Hunter RM was Mentioned in Dispatches.

TO THE
GLORY OF
GOD

AND IN
MEMORY
OF

THE OFFICERS AND MEN OF 41 INDEPENDENT
COMMANDO ROYAL MARINES WHO FELL
SERVING IN KOREA FROM SEPTEMBER 1950 TO
JUNE 1953 AND IN GRATITUDE FOR THOSE
WHO RETURNED. THIS TABLET IS ERECTED BY
MEMBERS OF THE CORPS FRIENDS & RELATIVES

CAPTAIN R.N. PARKINSON-CUMINE M.C. R.M.
LT J.G HARWOOD R.M.   MNE. S.E.H HILLS
SURG. LT D.A KNOCK MB BS RN   MNE. K.D. HITCHMAN
SGT C.E BARNES R.M.   MNE. W.L J JAUNCEY
A/P.O J.A TATE R.N.   MNE. P.R JONES
A/SGT R.G DAVIES R.M.   MNE. HARRY MELLING
CPL P.B BABB R.M.   MNE. JOSEPH McCOURT
CPL J.E BELSEY R.M.   MNE. R.J NEEDS
CPL C.R.B HILL R.M.   MNE. STANLEY SKELTON
CPL C.E TROTT R.M.   MNE. ERIC STRAIN
MNE. GERARD AHERN   MNE. D.W STRAY
MNE. A.J ALDRICH   MNE. W.A WALKER
MNE. IVAN GARNER   MNE. ROYSTON WOOLDRIDGE
MNE. J.L GRAHAM   MNE. KENNETH WYETH
MNE. L.A HEARD   MNE. REUBEN NICHOLLS
CPL. RONALD SOUTHWORTH   L/SBA DENNIS RAINES R.N.

GREATER LOVE HATH NO MAN THAN THIS
THAT A MAN LAY DOWN HIS LIFE FOR HIS FRIENDS

The Memorial Plaque in Bickleigh Parish Church, Devon